NOV 07 2013

ELK GROVE VILLAGE PUBLIC LIBRARY

S0-ARL-628

17

DISCARDED
Elk Grove Village
Public Library

ELK GROVE VILLAGE PUBLIC LIBRARY
1001 WELLINGTON AVE
ELK GROVE VILLAGE, IL 60007
(847) 439-0447

Essential Physical Science

ENERGY

Richard and Louise Spilsbury

Chicago, Illinois

© 2014 Heinemann Library
an imprint of Capstone Global Library, LLC
Chicago, Illinois

To contact Capstone Global Library, please
call 800-747-4992, or visit our web site,
www.capstonepub.com

All rights reserved. No part of this publication
may be reproduced or transmitted in any form
or by any means, electronic or mechanical,
including photocopying, recording, taping, or any
information storage and retrieval system, without
permission in writing from the publisher.

Edited by Nancy Dickmann, Adam Miller,
    and Diyan Leake
Designed by Victoria Allen
Original illustrations © Capstone Global
    Library Ltd 2014
Illustrated by H L Studios
Picture research by Ruth Blair
Originated by Capstone Global Library Ltd
Printed in China by CTPS

17 16 15 14 13
10 9 8 7 6 5 4 3 2 1

Library of Congress Cataloging-in-Publication Data
Spilsbury, Louise
  Energy / Louise and Richard Spilsbury.
    pages cm.—(Essential physical science)
  Includes bibliographical references and index.
  ISBN 978-1-4329-8144-0 (hb)—ISBN 978-1-4329-
8154-9 (pb) 1. Power resources—Juvenile literature.
2. Energy conversion—Juvenile literature. 3.
Renewable energy sources—Juvenile literature. I.
Spilsbury, Richard. II. Title.
  TJ163.23.S726 2014
  531'.6—dc23   2012051623

Acknowledgments
We would like to thank the following for permission
to reproduce photographs: Alamy pp. 11
(© Poelzer Wolfgang), 22 (© Brandon Cole Marine
Photography), 38 (© Global Warming Images);
Capstone Publishers (© Karon Dubke) pp. 12, 13,
24, 25, 40, 41; Corbis pp. 15 (© Bill Stormont), 31
(© Marc Müller/dpa), 32 (© Michael Rosenfeld/
Science Faction), 36 (© Ashley Cooper), 43
(© Laurent Gillieron/epa); Getty Images pp. 5 (Vegar
Abelsnes Photography), 6 (Sandra Mu), 10 (Dorling
Kindersley), 16 (Digital Vision), 18 (Steve Bonini),
21 (Oxford Scientific), 23 (Chip Somodevilla),
28 (Stuart Dee), 37 (Christian Aslund), 39 (Javier
Larrea), 42 (Environment Images/UIG); Science
Photo Library p. 19 (Power and Syred); Shutterstock
pp. 4 (© Bychkov Kirill Alexandrovich), 9 (© Yury
Zap), 14 (© steve estvanik), 17 (© Edyta Pawlowska),
20 (© Ozerov Alexander), 26 (© Khoroshunova
Olga), 29 (© eyeidea), 30 (© fotostory), 34
(© TonyV3112).

Cover photograph of an eruption of lava on Mount
Sakurajima, Japan, reproduced with permission of
Corbis (© Richard Roscoe/Stocktrek Images).

Every effort has been made to contact copyright
holders of material reproduced in this book. Any
omissions will be rectified in subsequent printings
if notice is given to the publisher.

Disclaimer
All the Internet addresses (URLs) given in this book
were valid at the time of going to press. However,
due to the dynamic nature of the Internet, some
addresses may have changed, or sites may have
changed or ceased to exist since publication. While
the author and publisher regret any inconvenience
this may cause readers, no responsibility for any
such changes can be accepted by either the author
or the publisher.

Contents

Eureka moment!

Learn about important discoveries that have brought about further knowledge and understanding.

DID YOU KNOW?

Discover fascinating facts about energy.

WHAT'S NEXT?

Read about the latest research and advances in essential physical science.

Some words are shown in bold, **like this**. You can find out what they mean by looking in the glossary.

What Is Energy?

Are you feeling full of energy? We cannot see energy, but we know what it does. Energy makes things happen or work. For example, it makes animals move, plants grow, eggs cook, lights glow, and car wheels spin, and it keeps homes warm.

Forms of energy

Energy is not all of the same form or type. For example, **chemical energy** is the energy stored within substances such as food or **fuels**. It is released after we eat or when we burn fuels. Another form is **mechanical energy**, which is the energy in the moving parts of machines such as jet engines. Other forms of energy are heat, sound, light, and **electrical energy**.

Energy is released when hot, melted rock from under the ground bursts from Earth's surface as a volcano erupts.

WHAT'S NEXT?

Scientists have developed a special type of black paper that can store electrical energy for when it is needed, like a **battery**. However, it is flexible and takes up very little space.

Where is energy from?

Energy comes from many natural sources. We get our energy to live from eating food—anything from bananas to salmon. The heat and light energy that keep our planet warm, and make green plants grow, comes from our nearest star, the Sun. We get lots of energy from burning natural fuels such as wood and coal, but some energy we use is from human-made sources. **Power stations** are special factories that use energy to make electricity.

Eureka moment!

In 1998, astronomers discovered a new, mysterious form of energy they called "dark energy." Dark energy is responsible for making all parts of the universe expand over time.

In this pizza oven, energy released by burning wood transfers to the dough and toppings to bake the ingredients together.

States of energy

Energy is all around us, and it is in everything. It is always either about to do something or actually doing something. These two states of energy are called **potential energy** and **kinetic energy**.

Potential energy is stored energy. A book resting on a high shelf has potential energy because it could fall from the shelf to the ground. A parked car has potential energy because the gasoline or diesel in its fuel tank could make the engine work. The working engine could make the wheels roll. Kinetic energy is energy that is actually working. A falling book and a speeding car both have kinetic energy.

DID YOU KNOW?

When fleas bend their back legs, rubbery tissue in their knees stores enough potential energy to allow them to jump 130 times their own height. That is like a person jumping over the Chrysler Building in New York City!

The British Paralympian Jonnie Peacock runs wearing a flexible carbon fiber blade on his right leg. The blade stores kinetic energy like a spring from when it strikes the track as potential energy. This energy drives the runner up and forward.

Amounts of energy

The amount of potential or kinetic energy is not always the same. For example, there is more potential energy when a fuel tank is full and when a book is on the highest shelf possible, because this could turn into more kinetic energy. Energy can easily change between states. For example, a roller coaster at the top of a hill has lots of potential energy. Some of this turns into kinetic energy as it speeds downhill. The roller coaster has less kinetic energy as it starts to climb the next hill, but more potential energy because it is getting higher.

Eureka moment!

In 1602, the Italian scientist Galileo observed that a swinging cathedral lamp always swung back to the same height it was released from. He realized that this was because the potential energy changed into kinetic energy, and back again.

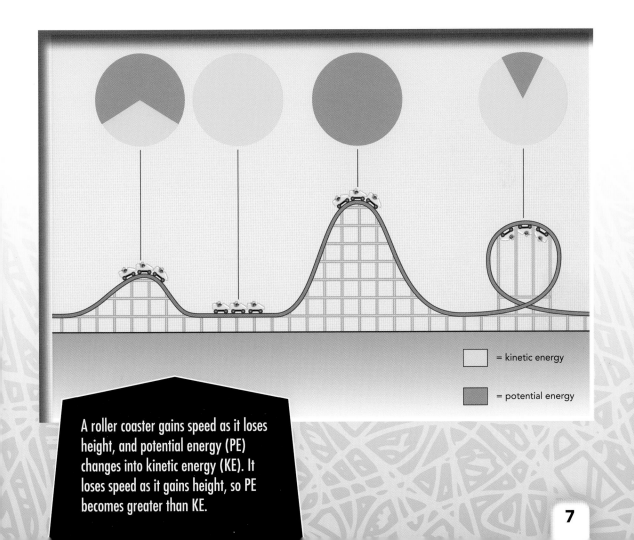

= kinetic energy

= potential energy

A roller coaster gains speed as it loses height, and potential energy (PE) changes into kinetic energy (KE). It loses speed as it gains height, so PE becomes greater than KE.

What Is Heat Energy?

We can get heat energy from many sources. For example, we get heat from the Sun, and our bodies create heat when we run around and exercise. Heating something up gives it heat energy. Cooling something down removes the heat energy from it.

Inside matter

All Earth's matter is made from tiny building blocks called **atoms**. Atoms are sometimes joined in groups called **molecules**. These particles are never completely still—they are always **vibrating** slightly. Adding heat energy to an atom or molecule makes it vibrate even more.

This diagram shows how water molecules are arranged in solids, liquids, and gases, and how states change when heat energy is added or taken away.

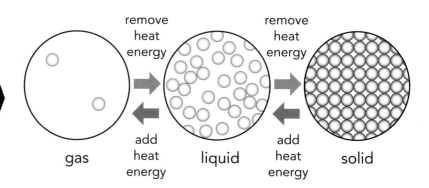

gas

remove heat energy

add heat energy

liquid

remove heat energy

add heat energy

solid

Eureka moment!

In 1945, Percy Spencer invented the microwave oven after noticing how microwave rays made a chocolate bar melt. Microwaves travel through food and make molecules vibrate, creating heat energy and warming food from the inside.

Changes in heat energy can make substances change from one form to another. For example, the water molecules in solid ice are tightly packed together, like marbles in a jar. When ice is heated, the molecules vibrate so much that they move and slide past each other. This melts the ice.

Adding yet more heat energy to water can make it evaporate and turn into vapor (gas). The molecules in a gas are spread out and move around in no particular arrangement. Cooling steam down slows the movement, so it **condenses**, or turns back into water. Removing even more heat energy makes the water molecules slow down and arrange themselves into ice.

These monkeys in Japan spend much of their time in hot springs, because the heat energy helps them stay warm on the snowy mountains where they live.

Moving heat

We need be careful when touching the handle of an iron pan on a stove because it can get hot. Heat spreads out from a warmer object or place to a colder one until both reach the same temperature. This is because when one atom or molecule is vibrating with heat energy, it can knock into other atoms or molecules around it until they are vibrating at the same speed. When heat travels from atom to atom through a material, it is called **conduction**. Some materials, such as metals, are better at conducting heat than others.

People handling very hot metal use long tongs to help protect their hands. The tongs can conduct heat, but each molecule in the tongs vibrates a little less the farther away it is from the source of heat energy.

WHAT'S NEXT?

Scientists have developed insulating materials called aerogels that conduct less heat than any other known substances. In the future, these could be used in anything from firefighters' suits to winter clothing.

Stopping conduction

Materials that do not conduct heat well are called insulators. Plastic and air are both insulators. Insulating materials help people and animals to stay warm in cold places. For example, whales and seals living in Arctic or Antarctic waters have a thick, fat insulation layer called blubber under their skin that stops them from getting too cold.

DID YOU KNOW?

The thickest natural insulation on any animal is the 17- to 19-inch (43- to 50-centimeter) layer of blubber on bowhead whales that live in the very cold Arctic Ocean.

Divers in icy water wear waterproof dry suits that stop cold water from entering the suit and trap air inside. The air has been heated by the divers' bodies. The suits prevents heat loss because air is a good insulator.

Try this!

Heat energy travels through different materials at different rates. Investigate which material is the best conductor of heat by experimenting with butter!

Prediction

Metal will conduct heat better than plastic or wood.

What you need

- A short wooden skewer
- A metal knife (same length as the skewer)
- A plastic knife (same length as the metal knife)
- A cup
- Very hot or boiling water
- Three ½-inch (1-centimeter) cubes from a block of butter or margarine,
- put in a refrigerator overnight
- A stopwatch
- A pencil
- Plain and graph paper

What you do

① Take the plastic knife and one cube of butter. Push the butter against one end of the knife until it sticks.

② Repeat for the wooden skewer and the metal knife.

③ Place the cup on a firm surface that will not be damaged if water spills. Ask an adult to carefully pour the hot or boiling water into the cup.

4 Have the pencil, paper, and stopwatch ready.

5 Very carefully, put the skewer and knives into the hot water, with the pieces of butter sticking out at the top. Make sure they are spread out so they are not touching. Do not touch the hot water. Start timing as soon as you put the objects into the water.

6 Carefully touch the skewer and the knives. Which feels hottest, and which is the coolest? Record when the butter starts to melt and slides or falls off.

Conclusion

Heat energy travels from the hot water up the skewer and knives and transfers to the butter, causing it to melt. The material that is the best heat conductor melts the butter the fastest. This should be the metal knife. Did your results match your prediction? You could try the experiment with different types of metals and other materials.

Heat circulation

Have you ever noticed that it can get hot upstairs in a house or building, even though the radiators are only on downstairs? Heat energy can move by **convection** as well as conduction. Convection is when moving molecules transfer heat energy through liquids or gases.

Air molecules around a hot radiator vibrate as they warm up. They then take up more space than cold air molecules, even though they stay the same weight. We say they have lower **density**. The hot air molecules by the radiator rise upward, and colder air with greater density moves into the space it has left. It then warms up. Rising warm air can push things upward—for example, soaring gliders and birds.

DID YOU KNOW?

The largest soaring land bird in the world is the Andean condor, with wings 11 feet (3.5 meters) across. It uses these huge wings to catch a lift on the hot air rising by convection.

Hot air balloons rise and float because the air inside is of lower density than that outside. This is achieved by heating air using burners underneath the balloon.

Heat waves

Heat energy can also be transmitted without the movement of atoms or molecules. **Radiation** is when heat energy is carried from something warm in invisible waves, or rays. For example, the Sun is 93 million miles (150 million kilometers) from Earth, but it warms our planet as its heat energy radiates through space. Toasters and grills cook food by radiation. Heat radiation is **absorbed** into dark or matte surfaces, but it **reflects** from shiny or light-colored surfaces.

WHAT'S NEXT?

In desert countries such as Namibia and Australia, people plan to build solar updraft towers. These are like large plastic greenhouses with tall chimneys. Air that is rising fast by convection can be used to generate electricity.

Shiny suits reflect away the heat energy radiating from fires and help stop firefighters from becoming too hot.

What Are Sound and Light Energy?

The noise and color of a stage musical are produced by sound and light energy. We can use sound and light energy to hear and see the world around us, for entertainment, and to communicate.

How sound works

Sound energy is a type of energy made by vibrations. For example, when someone sings, the surface of his or her throat vibrates in the air. The air molecules in the throat then vibrate. One molecule knocks into the next and so on, like the conduction of heat. This creates movements of air called **sound waves** that travel out of the singer's mouth.

Sound can only travel when there are molecules or atoms to knock into each other. This happens not only in air and other gases, but also in fluids such as water and in solids, including metal.

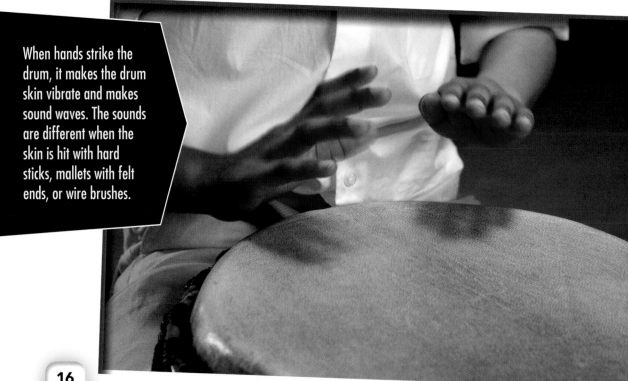

When hands strike the drum, it makes the drum skin vibrate and makes sound waves. The sounds are different when the skin is hit with hard sticks, mallets with felt ends, or wire brushes.

Hearing sound

Our ears allow us to sense sound waves. The outer ear is shaped like a funnel to send sound waves inside the ear. The waves hit the eardrum, which vibrates like a drum. Then parts of the inner ear convert the kinetic energy into signals of electrical energy. Our brains recognize these signals as sounds.

DID YOU KNOW?

A radio performer speaks into a microphone, creating sound waves. The waves are turned into radio waves. These are waves that can travel much farther through the air than sound waves. Then we can hear sounds made hundreds of miles away.

Sound waves of music are recorded and stored as electrical signals on an MP3 player. Earphones convert them back into sounds we can hear.

Light energy

Computer screens and candles are examples of objects that are luminous. This means they give off light energy. Light energy travels fast in waves, similar to heat radiation. Light waves can travel through transparent objects, such as glass windows, but are blocked by **opaque** objects, such as walls. Shadow is the area that light is blocked from on the other side of an opaque object.

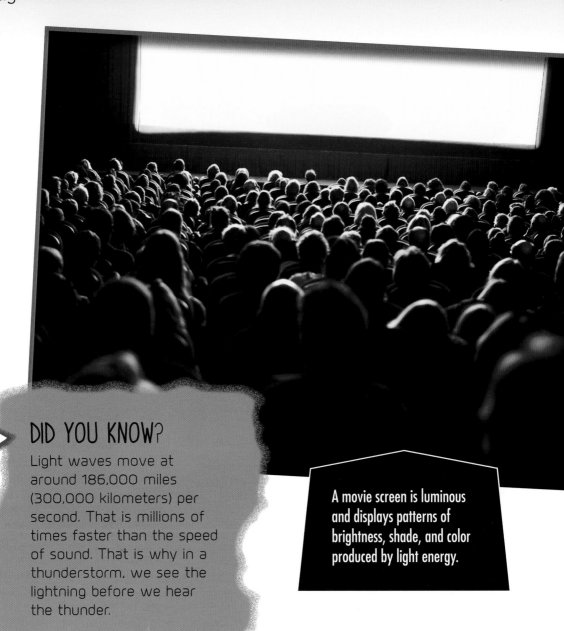

DID YOU KNOW?

Light waves move at around 186,000 miles (300,000 kilometers) per second. That is millions of times faster than the speed of sound. That is why in a thunderstorm, we see the lightning before we hear the thunder.

A movie screen is luminous and displays patterns of brightness, shade, and color produced by light energy.

Even in transparent objects, molecules can block and slow light waves. For example, light slows down when moving from air into water because the water has greater density. That is why a straw in water looks bent. The light energy from the part that is under the water moves to our eyes more slowly than the part above the surface. We say that the liquid **refracts** the light.

Eureka moment!

In 1970, American scientists developed fiber-optic cable. This is made of bundles of very thin glass strands that pulses of light can move through. These cables can carry more information much faster than copper wires.

Sight

Animals detect light energy through their eyes. Inside the eye is a layer called the retina. When light waves hit the retina, it converts light energy into electrical energy. This travels to the brain, which then interprets the electrical signals as images.

The large red eyes on this fly can detect things that change the light energy all around — for example, a moving fly swatter — so the fly can escape danger!

Light waves

A moving wave has high points, or peaks, and low points, or troughs. The distance between the peaks of the waves is called the **wavelength**. The different colors that make up light have different wavelengths. Sunlight may look white, but it is actually made up of lots of different colors. These colors make up what we call the **spectrum**. Each color in the spectrum has a different wavelength. Light at the red end of the spectrum has a longer wavelength than light at the violet end.

Rainbows are arcs of all the colors of the spectrum. They happen when beams of white sunlight hit raindrops in the sky at a certain angle. The white light then splits into the different colors of light.

Invisible parts of sunlight

The Sun gives off enormous amounts of energy, and some of this energy reaches Earth from space. The energy comes in many different wavelengths, but our eyes can only detect a certain range of these wavelengths as light. Other wavelengths are invisible. For example, ultraviolet radiation has a shorter wavelength than visible light, and **infrared radiation** has a longer wavelength.

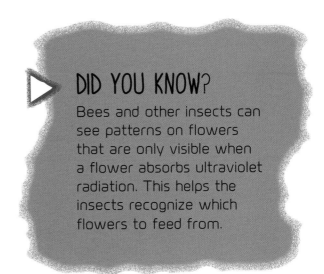

DID YOU KNOW?

Bees and other insects can see patterns on flowers that are only visible when a flower absorbs ultraviolet radiation. This helps the insects recognize which flowers to feed from.

We can detect these types of energy using tools, such as cameras, that are sensitive to these wavelengths. We can also see their effects. For example, our skin becomes damaged when it absorbs ultraviolet radiation from the Sun. We see this damage as sunburn.

Anything warm, not just the Sun, produces infrared radiation. We can see animals in the dark by using special goggles that can sense the infrared energy they give off.

What Is Chemical Energy?

Batteries, pasta, and gasoline are all common sources of energy. They (and many other substances) contain stored chemical energy. This form of energy is found in the links, or bonds, between the atoms that make up substances.

Releasing the energy

Bonds have a force that is similar to the pull of a weak magnet. The chemical energy in a bond is released when it is broken during a **chemical reaction**. These reactions happen when substances combine together to produce one or more new substances. In the reaction, some chemical energy is used to form new bonds between different atoms. For example, rust forms when iron reacts with oxygen. The original iron atoms remain, but they are bonded with oxygen, making iron oxide, or rust.

Squid use chemical reactions in their bodies to produce patterns of light. They might use this to attract animals that they then eat or to attract other squid that they may mate with.

Useful energy

Chemical energy is useful because it can be released when it is needed. For example, a fuel such as gasoline contains lots of chemical energy. Switching on a gasoline engine starts a burning reaction between gasoline and oxygen. This releases chemical energy as heat and also releases gases. The gases expand as they get warmer and push on sliding pistons. This movement can be used to make the wheels of a car turn. Batteries are stores of substances that release chemical energy as electrical energy when we put them in devices such as flashlights.

DID YOU KNOW?

In space, there is not enough oxygen in the **atmosphere** to burn rocket fuel. So, rockets carry their own supply stored in tanks so cold that the oxygen is liquid. This way, the oxygen takes up less space than its gas form.

The explosive power of a space rocket when it takes off is supplied when chemical energy in fuel is converted into kinetic energy.

Try this!

Some chemical reactions, including burning, release chemical energy as heat energy. These are called **exothermic reactions.** You can demonstrate an exothermic reaction using steel wool and vinegar.

What you need

- Steel wool
- Vinegar
- A plastic beaker
- A 4-inch (10-centimeter) square of aluminum foil with a hole poked through the center using the pencil
- A glass thermometer
- A stopwatch
- A measuring cup small enough to measure 1 fluid ounce (30 milliliters) accurately
- Paper and pencil
- Scissors
- Rubber gloves

What you do

1 Put the steel wool in the plastic beaker. Write down the temperature shown on the thermometer. Then gently push the thermometer (bulb side down) into the steel wool in the beaker. Seal the beaker by fitting the foil over the rim.

24

2 Start the stopwatch. After 5 minutes, remove the thermometer and record the temperature.

3 Remove the steel wool from the plastic beaker. Measure 1 fluid ounce (30 milliliters) of vinegar into the measuring cup and soak the steel wool in it for one minute. (The vinegar removes any oil from the wool.)

4 Wearing the gloves, squeeze the vinegar out of the steel wool pad.

5 Now repeat steps 1 and 2 and record the final temperature.

Conclusion

You should have recorded a temperature rise after the wool was soaked in vinegar. This is because the steel wool could not react with oxygen in the air around it with oil on its surface. After the vinegar had removed the surface oil, the steel could react. The heat energy released in this exothermic reaction made the temperature of the steel wool rise.

Food energy

Living things need food to supply chemical energy for movement and other life processes. Tiny cells are the building blocks of all living things. A chemical reaction called **respiration** inside cells converts glucose (a type of sugar) and oxygen into a chemical form of energy that cells can use. Carbohydrates such as pasta and bananas are rich in chemical energy because they are made up of lots of sugar molecules in chains. They give your cells plenty of fuel to turn into energy.

Animals have to eat food to obtain glucose. Green plants make their own glucose through a process in their leaves called **photosynthesis**. In photosynthesis, light energy from the Sun powers a chemical reaction between carbon dioxide and water to produce the glucose and oxygen gas.

Giant pandas eat mostly bamboo to supply the chemical energy they need. This energy originally came from sunlight used by the plant during photosynthesis.

Energy flow

Energy from the Sun is converted to chemical energy stored in plants during photosynthesis. Grazing animals such as gazelles take in some of this energy when they eat plants. Some energy is stored in their muscles and other tissues. A lion takes in this chemical energy when it eats the meat of the gazelle. The flow of energy, as one living thing eats another, is a process called a food chain.

WHAT'S NEXT?

In the future, people could be eating more seaweed and also feeding it to farm animals. Seaweed grows fast in oceans and other places where crops cannot. Apart from supplying chemical energy in food, seaweed can also supply fuel for vehicles!

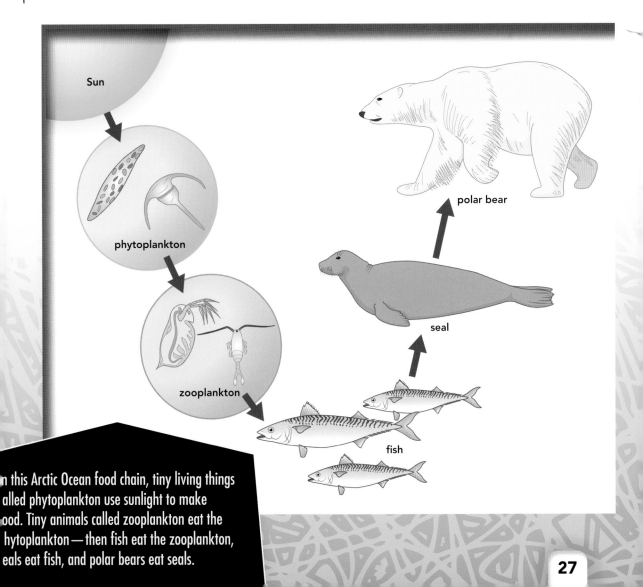

Sun

phytoplankton

zooplankton

fish

seal

polar bear

In this Arctic Ocean food chain, tiny living things called phytoplankton use sunlight to make food. Tiny animals called zooplankton eat the phytoplankton—then fish eat the zooplankton, seals eat fish, and polar bears eat seals.

How Do We Convert Fuels to Electricity?

Think of all the electrical appliances you and your family use every day, from lights to TVs. Electrical energy is one of the most common forms of energy we use. Most electrical energy is produced by using the chemical energy in fuels.

Electricity

When you turn on a light switch, electrical energy or electricity flows through wires to make a lightbulb glow. Electricity moves between atoms. Atoms have a central part called a **nucleus** with tiny particles called **electrons** whizzing around it. There is an **electrical current** when electrons flow from one atom to another, and so on.

Currents flow best in substances such as metals, where the electrons are loosest, so they can move easily. That is why most electrical wires are made from metal. The currents produce light, heat, sound, and other effects in different electrical appliances.

Electrical energy can be carried through metal wires (or cables) from where it is generated to where it is needed — for example, to light up cities.

Power fuels

Most electricity is made from burning coal or gas that has been dug out or drilled from underground. These two types of substances are called **fossil fuels** and are rich in chemical energy. Fossil fuels formed from the bodies of plants and animals that died millions of years ago. Over time, they were crushed underground and concentrated into fuels that are a source of chemical and potential energy.

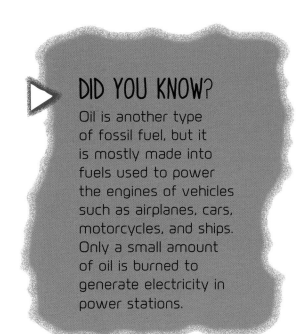

DID YOU KNOW?

Oil is another type of fossil fuel, but it is mostly made into fuels used to power the engines of vehicles such as airplanes, cars, motorcycles, and ships. Only a small amount of oil is burned to generate electricity in power stations.

Oil and gas are often found in rocks deep beneath the oceans. People build rigs that stand on the sea floor with long pipes to drill down to the buried fossil fuels and bring them to the surface.

Power stations

In a fossil-fuel power station, coal is broken into pieces or gas is mixed with air and then burned in a big furnace. This converts the chemical energy into heat energy. The heat boils water into very hot, fast-moving steam that pushes against special propellers called **turbines**. A pinwheel spins if you blow it—and steam makes the turbines spin in the same way, to convert kinetic energy in steam into mechanical energy. A device called a **generator** converts the spinning motion of the turbine into electrical energy.

Steam moves right from where it is made, and the turbine converts this into a spinning motion. The generator in a power station turns the spinning mechanical energy into electricity we can use.

WHAT'S NEXT?

In the future, there may be different nuclear reactors called fusion reactors. These can release even more nuclear energy by making the nuclei of hydrogen atoms stick to one another. This is the same process that happens on the Sun.

Atom power

Some power stations use **nuclear energy** to generate electricity. An atom's nucleus is held together by very powerful nuclear energy. In a special metal called uranium, the nucleus can be split open. The nuclear energy that is released converts to heat energy. Nuclear power stations have chambers called reactors where this nuclear reaction is controlled to generate electricity when people need it. Used nuclear fuel is hazardous because it produces invisible particles and waves that can make people sick. Nuclear waste needs to be handled and stored very carefully.

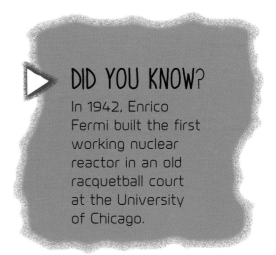

DID YOU KNOW?

In 1942, Enrico Fermi built the first working nuclear reactor in an old racquetball court at the University of Chicago.

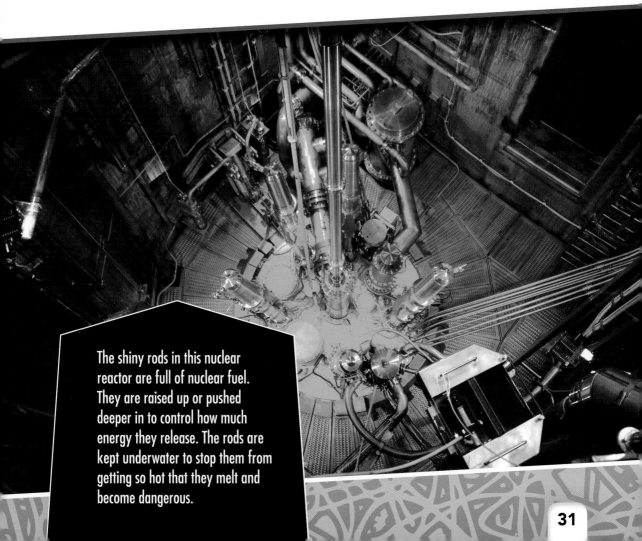

The shiny rods in this nuclear reactor are full of nuclear fuel. They are raised up or pushed deeper in to control how much energy they release. The rods are kept underwater to stop them from getting so hot that they melt and become dangerous.

Energy conversion

Imagine all the energy used worldwide as a fixed amount. When we use one form of energy, it does not disappear, but rather changes into a different form. For example, switching on a laptop converts some chemical energy in its battery into electrical energy, to make light energy for the display to work. With each change, some of the original energy is converted into forms of energy we cannot use or do not want, such as heat energy. If we use a laptop for a long time, the heat energy it releases goes into the air.

DID YOU KNOW?

Bikes are very energy-efficient machines. The amount of energy used to pedal a bike for 3 miles (5 kilometers) would only power an average car for 280 feet (85 meters).

When a moving metal cutter is used, it rubs on the surface of the metal, and lots of kinetic energy converts into heat energy. Oily liquid is poured on the cutter to reduce friction and keep the heat down.

Reducing energy loss

Reducing the amount of energy wasted in any machine is called energy efficiency. Only 40 percent of the chemical energy produced in a typical coal power station is turned into electrical energy. The remaining 60 percent of the energy from burning coal converts into heat energy. Some power stations are more energy efficient because they use the heat to warm water in buildings nearby. Energy-efficiency ratings on machines such as dishwashers help us choose those that use less electricity to carry out their job than others.

Eureka moment!

In 1847, James Joule measured the temperature of water in a waterfall above and below a paddle wheel. He found it was warmer below, proving that some of the mechanical energy in the wheel had converted into heat energy in the water.

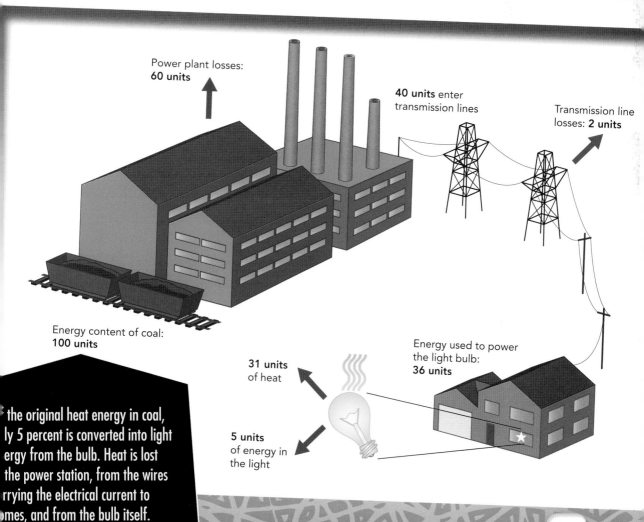

Power plant losses:
60 units

40 units enter transmission lines

Transmission line losses: **2 units**

Energy content of coal:
100 units

Energy used to power the light bulb:
36 units

31 units of heat

5 units of energy in the light

the original heat energy in coal, ly 5 percent is converted into light ergy from the bulb. Heat is lost the power station, from the wires rrying the electrical current to mes, and from the bulb itself.

What Is Renewable Energy?

People are trying to use fewer fossil fuels to generate electricity because fossil fuels cause environmental problems. Also, the fossil fuels we use today were formed over millions of years, and they are not being replaced. Eventually, our supplies will run out. Today, people are turning to **renewable energy** sources that will not run out. These include the Sun, wind, and moving water.

Atmospheric changes

Earth stays warm enough to live on because of the **greenhouse effect**. The Sun's energy warms up our planet. Some heat energy is absorbed, and some reflects back toward space. Gases in the atmosphere, including carbon dioxide, trap heat energy like a greenhouse. When fossil fuels are burned in machines, lots of carbon dioxide is released, in addition to energy. The carbon dioxide builds up in the atmosphere and traps more heat energy.

Earth's population is rising fast, and there is an increasing demand for fossil fuels to power machines such as cars.

Most scientists agree that the increased greenhouse effect is causing a gradual rise in average world temperatures. One effect of this is a change in weather patterns, which causes an increase of droughts and floods in some areas and makes it more difficult for people to grow food.

Eureka moment!

In 1896, the Swedish scientist Svante Arrhenius became the first person to predict that burning more fossil fuels would increase the greenhouse effect. He thought that it would happen slowly—and make his home country, Sweden, a warmer, more pleasant place to live!

WHAT'S NEXT?

People may start to mine the thick ice found in cold, deep oceans to get at the large amounts of ancient methane gas trapped inside, for use as a fuel. The problem is that mining could release lots of methane into the atmosphere. Methane traps more heat than carbon dioxide.

This diagram shows how the greenhouse effect works. The atmosphere traps heat energy that originally came from the Sun.

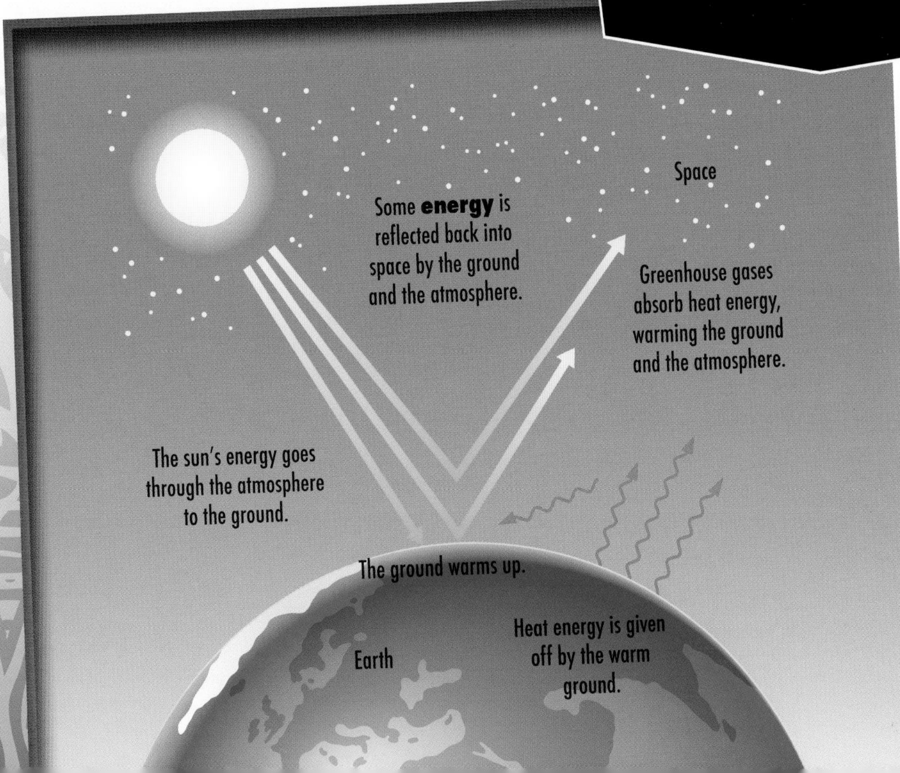

Space

Some **energy** is reflected back into space by the ground and the atmosphere.

Greenhouse gases absorb heat energy, warming the ground and the atmosphere.

The sun's energy goes through the atmosphere to the ground.

The ground warms up.

Earth

Heat energy is given off by the warm ground.

Water power

The most commonly used renewable energy is moving water, which generates one-fifth of global electricity. **Hydroelectric power** uses water that flows naturally down rivers, or that is released into channels from water trapped in reservoirs, which are huge basins that contain the water behind dams. The water spins turbines and generators, just like the steam in a coal-fired plant. Wave power uses the force of waves moving across oceans. Tidal power uses the flow of seawater to spin turbines and generators when tides rise and fall.

DID YOU KNOW?

The largest hydroelectric reservoir in the world is at the Three Gorges Dam in China. Its reservoir (which contains the water to activate its turbines) is longer than Lake Superior. The dam can generate as much electricity as 10 nuclear power stations.

This giant floating structure is called Pelamis. Its hinged sections move with the rise and fall of ocean waves. Machines inside convert this kinetic energy into electricity.

Wind power

People harvest the power of wind by using wind turbines. These are large propellers that spin when moving air hits their blades. The turbines are raised on tall towers that are often positioned on hills or out at sea. This is because wind blows faster high above the ground and across flat stretches of ocean where there are fewer obstacles, such as trees or buildings. With more kinetic wind energy, the blades can spin faster and generate more electricity. When the wind drops, the turbines cannot generate electricity.

WHAT'S NEXT?

New styles of wind turbines are being developed. These are tied to long cables from Earth, like kites, that are high up in the sky, where winds are strongest.

One turbine produces a small amount of electricity compared with a power station. On wind farms, several turbines are positioned together in order to generate more electricity.

Solar power

Globally, only about 1 percent of electricity is generated from the Sun's energy. There are two main ways to do this. In a solar thermal power station, mirrors reflect heat from the Sun onto tubes containing a liquid. The liquid can get very hot, and this heat energy is transferred to water in separate tubes. The water boils, and the steam turns turbines and generators.

In this solar thermal power station, there are 600 mirrors angled to reflect the Sun's heat onto a tower, where it is used to generate electricity.

Another way that electricity can be generated directly from sunlight is by using **photovoltaic cells**. A substance in these cells, called silicon, converts light energy into electrical energy. Many cells, each generating a small current, are usually connected together in solar panels to produce larger currents.

Eureka moment!

In 1883, Charles Fritts made the first photovoltaic cell from gold leaf and a material called selenium. His cell was expensive, and it was 40 times less energy-efficient than today's most efficient cells.

Hot rock power

Another renewable energy source is geothermal power. The center of Earth is 600 times hotter than boiling water. A few miles beneath Earth's surface, the rock is so hot in some places that water can be pumped underground to make steam to generate electricity or to heat buildings.

WHAT'S NEXT?

Iceland has so much geothermal energy that it plans to build a 745-mile (1,200-kilometer) underwater cable to sell spare electricity from geothermal power stations to other parts of Europe. It will be the longest cable in the world.

There is hot underground rock near the surface in New Zealand and Iceland. This makes geothermal power an important source of energy for heating water.

Try this!

You can conduct your own experiment to demonstrate the power of solar energy. However, you will need to carry this out on a hot, sunny day for best results!

Prediction

Concentrating solar energy can increase heat energy.

What you need

- A shoebox without a lid
- A bamboo barbecue skewer, longer than the length of the box
- Aluminum foil
- Sticky tape
- A small sheet of thin cardboard the size of printer paper or a manila folder

- String
- Marshmallows
- A ruler
- Scissors

What you do

1 Using the ruler, measure the height and width of the shoebox at one end. Mark a vertical line from the top of the box that is half the height of the box and positioned midway across the end of the box. Repeat at the other end.

2 Carefully cut out a slot the width of the skewer down each line. The skewer will be positioned between these slots.

3 Cut the manila folder in half along the fold. Place one half (or the sheet of cardboard) into the box so it drapes curved into a half-pipe shape resting on the bottom of the box. Use tape to stick it into the box.

40

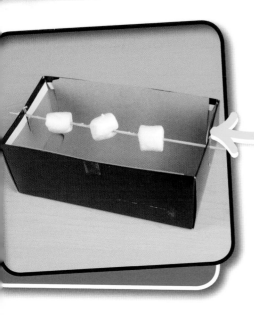

4 Carefully push three marshmallows onto the skewer and rest it between the slots.

5 Place the box outside in direct sunlight. Start the stopwatch. How long does it take for the marshmallows to melt onto the cardboard dish?

6 Now remove the skewer and cover the cardboard and inner ends of the box with aluminum foil, with the shiny surface facing upward. Hold it in place using tape. Repeat steps 4 and 5.

Conclusion

You should find that the curved cardboard on its own absorbs too much heat energy to warm the marshmallows. By adding reflective material (aluminum foil) to the cardboard, sunlight and heat reflect onto the marshmallows from the sides and below. The concentrated heat energy then cooks the marshmallows. Enjoy!

Stay safe!

Light, as well as heat, is concentrated by the aluminum foil in this demonstration. Never look at the light or put your head near the center of the box, because this could damage your eyes.

Is Energy Use Changing?

Energy is essential for all living things to survive. However, the ways we have found to convert energy into the forms we need have allowed humans to transform their lives. For example, we have developed important machines such as airplanes, generators, lightbulbs, and computers.

However, demand for fuel and electricity is rising. This is partly because the global population is getting bigger, people are increasingly traveling by fuel-powered vehicles, and we have far more electrical gadgets than we did in the past.

Energy solutions

Scientists are working to develop alternative fuels that do not make the greenhouse effect worse. For example, fuel cells are special batteries that can power vehicles. They use the reaction between hydrogen and oxygen to convert chemical energy into electrical energy, with water, rather than carbon dioxide, as waste. Biofuels are fuels that are processed from crops such as corn. They release less carbon dioxide than oil as they burn. However, they need a lot of space and massive amounts of water to grow, and they use a lot of energy when being processed into fuels.

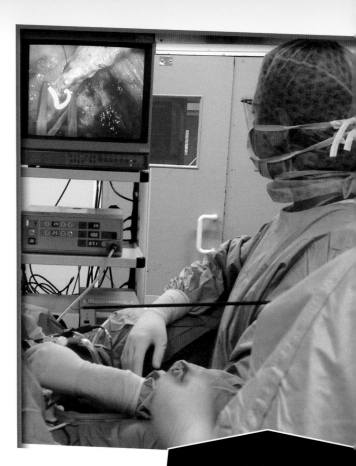

Many medical procedures use electrical machines. This doctor is using special electronic devices to carry out surgery deep inside a patient.

The other energy solution is to use less. For example, people can walk and cycle, share rides, or take public transportation rather than drive cars. They can reuse goods such as secondhand clothes rather than buying new ones that use up energy when they are made in factories.

Eureka moment!

In 1839, a Welsh judge and inventor named William Grove invented the first fuel cell that combined hydrogen and oxygen to make electricity and water.

One way to reduce our use of oil is to use renewable alternatives to power vehicles. This airplane uses photovoltaic cells on top of the wings to power its engines and propellers.

WHAT'S NEXT?

In the future, we could all be wearing clothes made of special fabric that generates electricity as we move around!

Glossary

absorb take something in—for example, a sponge absorbs water

atmosphere layer of gases that surround Earth

atom smallest part of a substance that can take part in a chemical reaction. Everything from cells to sand is made from different atoms.

battery store of chemical energy used to release electrical energy to power electrical devices

chemical energy type of energy in chemical substances that joins atoms or molecules together

chemical reaction when the atoms in different things react with each other and change

condense change from gas to liquid form—for example, when steam turns to water, usually by cooling

conduction movement of heat energy through a material

convection when molecules in a gas or liquid change density, so that the lighter parts rise and the denser parts sink

density measure of the weight of a substance compared with the volume it takes up. For example, steam has lower density than water.

electrical current flow or movement of electricity

electrical energy type of energy created by the movement of electrons; also called electricity

electron very small part of an atom, it has a negative electric charge

exothermic reaction chemical reaction that releases heat energy into its surroundings

fossil fuel fuel such as coal or oil that was formed from plants or animals that died millions of years ago

fuel material containing lots of chemical or nuclear energy that can be released as heat energy for use in powering machines

generator machine that converts mechanical energy into electrical energy

greenhouse effect when heat energy from the Sun is trapped in the atmosphere by gases such as carbon dioxide

hydroelectric power generating electricity using kinetic energy from moving water

infrared radiation type of energy produced by the Sun and other warm objects with a wavelength longer than visible light

kinetic energy movement energy

mechanical energy kinetic energy that can move parts in a machine

molecule group of two or more atoms

nuclear energy type of energy produced from atoms of special metals

nucleus (plural: **nuclei**) central part of a cell that controls how it works

opaque material through which light cannot pass

photosynthesis process in the leaves of plants that uses the Sun's energy to make glucose from carbon dioxide and water

photovoltaic cell device that converts energy in sunlight into electrical energy

potential energy energy that could do work, such as stored energy in fuel or water stored above the ground

power station factory where electricity is made

radiation movement of energy, such as heat or light, in straight lines that spread out as they travel from the source

reflect bend or throw back light

refract light rays that bend when they pass at an angle from one kind of material (such as water) to another (such as air)

renewable energy energy from a source such as wind or moving water that can be used without running out

respiration process in living things that releases energy from food

sound wave vibration in a medium such as air or water that we hear as sound

spectrum band of different colored lights in order of their wavelength

turbine machine that is powered by pressure from steam, water, or wind

vibrate move up and down, or back and forth, very quickly

wavelength distance between two crests of a wave

Find Out More

Books

Biskup, Agnieszka. *Aliens and Energy* (Monster Science). Mankato, Minn.: Capstone, 2012.

Challoner, Jack. *Energy* (DK Eyewitness Books). New York: Dorling Kindersley, 2012.

Chambers, Catherine. *Energy in Crisis* (Protecting Our Planet). New York: Crabtree, 2010.

Krohn, Katherine. *A Refreshing Look at Renewable Energy with Max Axiom, Super Scientist* (Graphic Science). Mankato, Minn.: Capstone, 2010.

Solway, Andrew. *The Scientists Behind Energy* (Sci-Hi). Chicago: Raintree, 2011.

Web sites

www1.eere.energy.gov/kids
This web site is all about kids saving energy, including some simple facts about renewable energy.

www.eia.gov/kids/energy.cfm?page=1
This web site explores energy, renewable and nonrenewable sources of energy, and the history of energy, and it has some games and activities.

www.energyhog.org/childrens.htm
This is a fun interactive web site that helps us to think about ways to use less electricity, with the help of characters called energy hogs—which can spot wasted energy in lots of different places.

www.ndt-ed.org/EducationResources/HighSchool/Electricity/workwithelectricity.htm
This interactive web site explains electricity.

Places to visit

American Museum of Science and Energy
300 S. Tulane
Oak Ridge, Tennessee 37830
amse.org

This museum offers fun exhibits and hands-on activities that explore energy in many different forms, including renewable energy and nuclear energy.

Exploratorium
Pier 15
San Francisco, California 94111
www.exploratorium.edu

This museum examines many different aspects of science, including energy, and offers hands-on activities.

Further research

Wind turbines do not turn when the wind is not blowing. Research some of the other problems with different forms of renewable energy and how people are solving them.

Research what these terms mean: *fracking*, *clathrates*, *tar sands*, *Arctic oil*.

Find out more about energy companies and how they are trying to find enough fossil fuels for the world to use.

Research more about energy-saving transportation options for the future, such as solar-powered cars, boats, and airplanes. You can also research ways to save energy in homes and businesses.

Index